God,
Me,
and
Coffee

"You prepare a table before me in the presence of my enemies.

You anoint my head with oil; my cup overflows."

(Psalm 23:5)

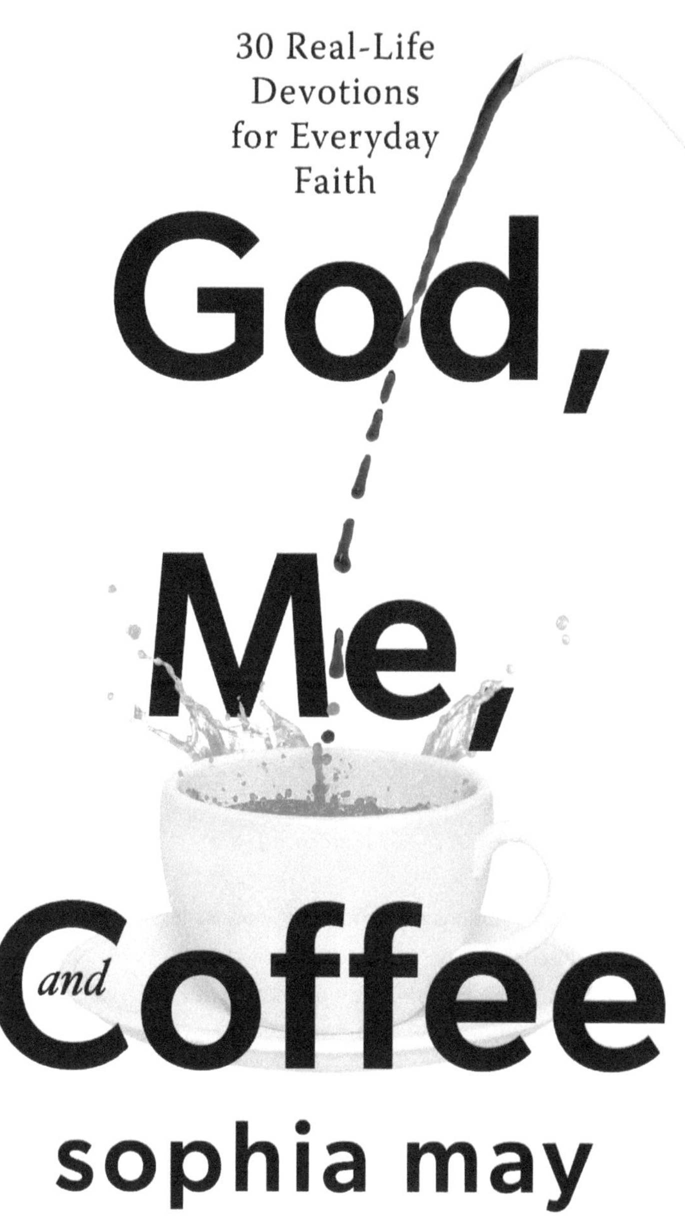

30 Real-Life
Devotions
for Everyday
Faith
God,
Me,
and Coffee
sophia may

ISBN:979-8-9950771-1-4 (Paperback)
ISBN: 979-8-9950771-0-7 (Hardcover)

Front cover image © Shutterstock.com.
Book design by Alan Hebel.

First printing edition 2026.

Dedication

To Mum and Dad, thank you for planting God's Word deep in my heart. Your legacy lives on through every page. I love you.

To my darling husband, who has read every devotion, believed in every dream, and encouraged every leap of faith: thank you for our beautiful life together.

To my sisters and sisters-in-law, thank you for cheering me on and daring me to dream big. Ann, thank you to you and your prayer group for encouraging me to carry on.

And to my pastor and church family: Thank you for seeing a gift in me I didn't see and encouraging me to keep writing. It's because of all of your encouragement, our community, and our heart for God that I wrote this book and continue to write.

Contents

A Note from the Author

"I have hidden your word in my heart that I might not sin against you."

(Psalm 119:11)

I didn't set out to become a devotional writer. It all began when my pastor asked me to contribute to a collection of devotions for Lent. I remember sitting at my living room table, finishing a puzzle with my youngest daughter, and thinking, *What exactly am I going to write?* And so I wrote "Puzzle Pieces."

I grew up as a preacher's daughter, so Scripture was woven into my life every day at dinner, at bedtime, and on Sundays in church. These Scripture verses are still tucked in my heart today. I wanted to capture them in my devotions in a real and relatable way so anyone could understand them, even people who are on the fence about their faith and have questions about God. God shows up in our lives in many ways, not just on Sundays and at Easter, Christmas, weddings, and funerals. He is with us all the time, and I wanted to illustrate that in this book.

So grab your favorite drink (coffee for me) and settle in for a few minutes each day. I pray that somewhere in these pages you find encouragement, hope, and a reminder that God is always present, always loving, and always writing your story.

Section 1

Come As You Are

God delights in every part of your life, even the silly, imperfect, and mundane parts. He takes joy in all of it.

1. Puzzle Pieces

"'For I know the plans I have for you,' declares the Lord, 'plans to prosper you and not to harm you, plans to give you hope and a future.'"

(Jeremiah 29:11)

My daughter and I have a passion for puzzles that began when she was just four years old. She started with simple twenty-piece puzzles, then moved on to hundred-piece ones when she turned five. Now, at six, we're tackling five- and six-hundred-piece puzzles together. Although it can be frustrating and take days, it's our bonding time, and there's no greater satisfaction than when the puzzle is complete.

Starting a new puzzle, though, is always the hardest part for both of us. The pieces are scattered everywhere, and even with the final picture on the box, I feel hopeless. The pieces don't seem to fit, and I'll even think pieces are missing and ask my daughter to look on the floor. On occasion, we've had to take breaks and work on puzzles for days before they start to come together.

Have you ever felt this way in your walk with God? You have a sense of what the final picture should look like, but you have no idea how it will come together, and you've felt hopeless. Maybe what you've been praying for feels far off, and God gives you only a small piece of the whole picture. You feel weary, burdened, and uncertain of what to do next. Maybe you have cried and questioned or even doubted God. Meanwhile, your loved ones are telling you, "You've got this."

Maybe it's been months since you applied for that university placement, and you didn't get the result you wanted. Maybe a job offer or promotion hasn't come, and you've been working hard. Or perhaps a romantic relationship hasn't progressed to the next level. But just as the puzzle pieces slowly fall into place, so, too, is God at work in your life. He holds the big picture and works in His perfect timing. Trust that even when you can't see it all yet, God is making it fit together.

Remember, it's okay to take a break and come back to whatever you are working on and praying for until tomorrow. God is working on it.

Prayer

God, help me to believe that the pieces of my life will fit together exactly the way You have designed them. Amen.

2. Shopping Cart

"Consider it pure joy, my brothers and sisters, whenever you face trials of many kinds, because you know that the testing of your faith produces perseverance. Let perseverance finish its work so that you may be mature and complete, not lacking anything."

(James 1:2–4)

Saturday grocery trips with my mum were the highlight of my week. Bright aisles filled with fruit, tea, fresh bread, and the best biscuits were our happy place. It was a simple tradition that felt like pure joy.

Years later, I noticed the motorized shopping carts at the store and immediately thought of my mother-in-law. She has struggled with mobility, and I longed to create new memories with her, filled with laughter and choosing snacks we didn't need. But each time I suggested the cart, she politely refused.

Then one quiet Thursday evening, she finally said yes.

A little nervous, she eased onto the cart, placed her hands on the controls, and then she was off! She confidently navigated the store with a smile that lit up her whole face. I stood there watching, realizing God had allowed joy to return in a completely new way.

The Scripture passage in James 1:2–4 reminds us that trials aren't the absence of joy; instead, they are often the soil where perseverance grows. Seasons of loss, limitations, or waiting can feel heavy, yet God is quietly preparing surprising blessings ahead. When joy returns even in a grocery store, it reminds us that His goodness never runs out.

Reflection

Where in your life might God be preparing a new kind of joy, even in a situation that has felt difficult or disappointing?

3. Watermelon Sugar

"There is a time for everything, and a season for every activity under the heavens."
(Ecclesiastes 3:1)

Each season of life brings its own rhythm, its own beauty, its own challenges, its own purpose. In our family, we've learned to lean into those rhythms with traditions that help us pause, savor, and give thanks for God's provision.

One of our favorite summer traditions is making watermelon juice. It's simple watermelon, ginger, mint, lime, and a little brown sugar but it's so much more than a drink. It's the kids cutting watermelon and eating more than they contribute, and me wondering why I always end up with less juice and more mess than the day before. It's the whirl of the blender, the taste-testing, and tweaking: more lime? more ginger? just a touch more sugar? It's that first icy sip on a hot day, the moment we declare: *summer is here!*

In a world that pushes us to rush into the next thing, traditions like these slow us down. They remind us to enjoy the sweetness God places in every season to laugh, to build memories, to share joy with those we love, and to carry that joy into the seasons that bring change.

As each season flows into the next, let's embrace the new rhythm, knowing that God has a purpose for every season, and each one arrives right on time.

Reflection

What simple tradition helps you slow down and notice God's goodness in your current season?

4. Potluck

"Each of you should give what you have decided in your heart to give, not reluctantly or under compulsion, for God loves a cheerful giver."

(2 Corinthians 9:7)

Roasted turkey. Cranberry stuffing. Candied yams. Mac and cheese. String beans. Chocolate flan. Curried chicken. Potato salad. Coquito. Paneer tikka masala. Christmas rice. Spinach dip. The list went on.

Our office potluck looked like the United Nations gathered around a table, every dish telling the story of someone's home, culture, and history. As each person placed their dish down, I could feel the heart, love, and tenderness that went into preparing it. This wasn't just food. It was generosity layered with family memories, rich flavors, and childhood stories.

Scripture is full of people who brought offerings to God sacrifices that came from the heart. Some gave food or livestock. Some gave all they had. Abraham was even willing to offer Isaac. Each gift was an act of worship expressing gratitude, devotion, and repentance.

Paul echoes this truth. A gift is judged not by its

size but by the posture of the heart: joyful, willing, and freely given.

Most of the people at our potluck weren't giving to God, yet their cheerful giving still reflected God's heart. At one shared table across different cultures, beliefs, and backgrounds, generosity became a bridge to connection.

Reflection

Where might God be inviting you to give your time, talent, or treasure to someone new?

5. First-Class Faith

"He raises the poor from the dust and lifts the needy from the ash heap; he seats them with princes and has them inherit a throne of honor."

(1 Samuel 2:8)

When I was a child, flying felt like a luxury experience. My mother would dress us up before every long-haul flight and say, "If we look presentable and behave well, and if there's space in First Class, we might be blessed with an upgrade." I believed her wholeheartedly. I sat tall, crossed my legs like a little lady, and imagined silver cutlery, warm towels, unlimited orange juice, and stacks of coloring books waiting for me at the front of the plane.

Most times, we stayed right where our tickets were in Economy Class but that hope stayed with me. What fascinated me wasn't the seat itself but the idea that one day, if I worked really hard, my mum and I could sit together in First Class.

Many of us still carry quiet dreams of First-Class moments in our careers, relationships, finances, fitness goals, or personal growth. But life can often feel more like Economy seating: cramped, functional, and limited. We tell ourselves we should simply be grateful to be on the plane at all.

In 1 Samuel 2:8, we see that God is not intimidated by humble beginnings or unlikely candidates. He specializes in divine upgrades not because of status, performance, or perfection, but because of His purpose and power.

Sarah gave birth to her first son at ninety. Abraham was promised to be the father of many nations when he was well into old age. Joseph was betrayed, sold into slavery, imprisoned, and forgotten. But when God writes the story, the final chapter never looks like the first.

Today, whether you feel like you are sitting in the front, the middle, or the back of life's plane, remember this: faith is your boarding pass, and God decides the timing. No one else can take the seat He has assigned to you.

Reflection

Where in your life do you need to trade Economy expectations for First-Class faith?

6. Lettuce and Water

"Forget the former things; do not dwell on the past. See, I am doing a new thing! Now it springs up; do you not perceive it?"

(Isaiah 43:18–19)

Lately, my oldest daughter has taken an interest in science. Her curiosity has sparked something beautiful in our home: small experiments, big questions, and a renewed sense of wonder at how the world works. One of her latest projects left me both gobsmacked and reflective. She cut off the root of an iceberg lettuce and placed it in a glass of water on our sunny windowsill.

A week later, something incredible happened: that discarded, brown-looking root began to sprout new lettuce. The lettuce was bright green!

It instantly brought to mind God's promise in Isaiah: "See, I am doing a new thing!"

How often do we carry old habits, toxic relationships, or seemingly harmless distractions that quietly take root in our lives? They might offer fleeting comfort, but over time, they begin to drain our energy, our joy, and even our sense of self. Still, we hold on. Letting go is rarely easy; it often comes with uncertainty, grief, and discomfort.

But God reminds us to forget the former things. Not because they never mattered, but because they no longer define our future. Something new, something better, brighter, and fresher is waiting to grow, just like those unexpected green leaves pushing up from the old root. Maybe for you, cutting off looks like letting go of a habit you've quietly struggled with for years. It might be creating distance from a relationship that consistently drains your peace. Or it might be setting boundaries with your phone or laptop at home so you can be more fully present with those you love. Whatever it is, know this: God is doing something new.

Reflection

Where have you seen God start something new in your life when you have cut off something old?

Section 2

Trust and Believe

"Now faith is confidence in what we hope for and assurance about what we do not see" (Hebrews 11:1). Our belief turns into something we could never imagine if we trust in God.

7. Mustard Seed

"He told them another parable: 'The kingdom of heaven is like a mustard seed, which a man took and planted in his field. Though it is the smallest of all seeds, yet when it grows, it is the largest of garden plants and becomes a tree, so that the birds come and perch in its branches.' "

(Matthew 13:31–32)

As a child, I loved this Scripture passage. I would picture how tiny a mustard seed was barely visible, like a speck, and I couldn't comprehend how something so miniature could become something so great. It was inconceivable to me then. But as I've grown and matured and have had the privilege of seeing some of my dreams realized—finding my husband, watching my family grow, and seeing my loved ones grow and thrive—I now understand how the smallest of seeds can become the largest of trees.

Have you ever thought about the mustard seeds that others plant in you through their words?

Scripture reminds us that "the tongue has the power of life and death, and those who love it will eat its fruit" (Proverbs 18:21). Sometimes, a single word of encouragement can plant a seed that blooms into greatness.

Maybe someone saw something in you that you couldn't yet see in yourself. Maybe they recognized a gift or a strength, and they encouraged you to explore it and reach for the stars. Or perhaps you were the one planting seeds. Maybe you were the basketball coach and you planted the seed in your players, urging them to trust their teammates and take that final shot. Or maybe you coached your coworker to lead a team meeting, encouraging them to speak up and share their ideas.

And then, there's the other side: the times when we planted seeds unknowingly, through careless or discouraging words. Such words may have taken root in someone's heart and caused them to doubt their worth or purpose.

The truth is that we are constantly planting mustard seeds in others through our words, actions, encouragement, and even silence. Seeds have the power to grow into something inconceivably great or something we never intended.

So today, let's be intentional about the seeds we sow. May our words breathe life. May our encouragement nurture hidden potential. And may we never underestimate the power of something small, because with God, even the tiniest seed can become the greatest of trees.

Reflection

What encouraging seed can you plant in someone today? Where is God nudging you to take a bold, mustard-seed step of faith?

8. Don't Worry

"Look at the birds of the air; they do not sow or reap or store away in barns, and yet your heavenly Father feeds them. Are you not much more valuable than they?"

(Matthew 6:26)

Anxiety. It's a familiar visitor in our lives, showing up in our homes, at work, and even in quiet conversations with friends. Not long ago, admitting you felt anxious or overwhelmed was taboo. You kept moving through life, and you kept it private. But today, between the relentless news cycle, natural disasters, global pandemics, political unrest, and grocery prices, stress feels like it comes standard.

Here's what hasn't changed: God. He is still the same yesterday, today, and forever. Still in control. Still providing. Still present. Still answering prayers.

In Matthew 6:26, Jesus offers a gentle reminder: Look at the birds. They don't sow or store away, and yet they're fed daily. And you, yes, you are far more valuable to Him.

Living this truth isn't always easy. My own worries aren't always about the big things. Sometimes, it's as small as figuring out dinner on a Wednesday night. I'll sigh to my husband, "What are we going to eat tomorrow?" And without hesitation, he smiles and says, "Tomorrow will take care of itself. Look at the birds."

Whether it's a heavy burden or a simple daily stress, the invitation is the same: Look at the birds. If God provides for them, how much more will He provide for you? We don't need to carry tomorrow's weight today. We can rest in His care, trusting that He will provide.

Prayer

God, I cast all my cares on You. Please take care of this heavy burden. If You can do it for the birds of the air, I believe You can do it for me. Amen.

9. A Glass of Water

"But whoever drinks the water
I give them will never thirst. Indeed,
the water I give them will become
in them a spring of water welling
up to eternal life."

(John 4:14)

I recently had dinner with a close friend who is expecting her second child. I was so thrilled to see her blossoming. She had just ten weeks to go before her son would be born, and we couldn't have been more excited. As we sat down in the restaurant, we both ordered a tall glass of water to cool off. She looked at the glass, drank it, and then paused thoughtfully.

"Have you ever thought about how water can shapeshift?" she asked. "Right now, it's quenching my thirst. But it can also become ice to cool us down, or steam to help us cook. It's the same substance, just showing up in different ways, in just the right way we need, no matter the circumstances."

Her words stayed with me. I thought about how God's presence moves in our lives: sometimes it's refreshing and direct, like a cool drink, while at other times it's subtle and purifying, like steam, or firm and preserving, like ice.

As a mom, there are times when I'm gentle and soft, like when my kids need comfort after a fall in the playground. At other times, I need to be firm, like when homework is incomplete or when the bedrooms are untidy.

Like water, our heavenly Father meets us in many forms: in comfort during grief, in guidance during confusion, in strength during weakness. Always the same God. Always near. Always able to quench our deepest thirst, just like a tall glass of water at dinner with a friend.

Prayer

Lord, thank You for meeting every need in just the right way and at just the right time. Help me see Your presence in every season, even in the seasons that are dark and difficult. Help me to believe that You are always providing living water for my soul. Amen.

10. You're Gorgeous

**"Abraham fell facedown;
he laughed and said to himself,
'Will a son be born to a man a
hundred years old? Will Sarah bear
a child at the age of ninety?' "**

(Genesis 17:17)

It's only now, past my twenties and thirties, that I notice how obsessed we are with staying young. Everywhere I look, society tells us wrinkles are mistakes, gray hairs are flaws, and aging is something to hide. But what if society celebrated growing older as something beautiful? With age comes wisdom, confidence, a strength that allows us to stand firm in our beliefs, and freedom in being ourselves.

Recently, I met up with a friend who was considering a cosmetic procedure. She told me that everyone was doing it and it was the norm. I looked at her with love and care, and all I could see was beauty.

I didn't want to judge, and I could see how much this meant to her and would make her happy, so I said, "You're gorgeous as you are. But if it will make you happy, and it's what you want to do, I think it's great."

Sarah was over ninety years old when God told her she would be a mother. Can you imagine the scandal this must have caused at the time? She was certainly too old to be a mother and perhaps even too old to be a grandmother. Sarah must have had wrinkles and gray hair. Yet God did not see her age or imperfections; He saw her beauty, her fertility, and her readiness to begin something new.

With God's grace and mercy, we can bring forth new life, start new careers, nurture new relationships, explore new hobbies, and embrace new desires. We are never too old to begin something new.

Prayer

God, help me to love myself the way You love me. Teach me that I am never too old, too late, or too far behind to begin something new. Amen.

11. In Someone Else's Shoes

"So in everything, do to others what you would have them do to you, for this sums up the Law and the Prophets. Enter through the narrow gate. For wide is the gate and broad is the road that leads to destruction, and many enter through it. But small is the gate and narrow the road that leads to life, and only a few find it."

(Matthew 7:12–14)

It's said that CEOs who rise through the ranks from entry level to executive often lead with greater empathy and compassion. Their firsthand experiences make them more understanding of others. It's an interesting concept, but I'm not entirely convinced. I've known people who built their own businesses from scratch, with no prior experience, and they still lead with great empathy and compassion. They can't always empathize with every single employee and don't have firsthand experience in each position, but they do their very best to listen and learn, and they embrace humility.

While experience can certainly teach compassion, empathy doesn't require us to have lived every story. Being kind and considerate toward others isn't reserved for those who have "been there." More often, empathy is a conscious choice: a willingness to pause, to listen, and to imagine what someone else might be feeling, even when their journey looks nothing like our own. It's choosing not to judge by our own standards or circumstances.

That isn't easy. Human nature is inclined to focus on itself: our own challenges, needs, and perspective. It can be hard to relate to those whose experiences differ from ours, people of different backgrounds, races, genders, or faiths, or those who live in different communities or follow different career paths. Yet in His Sermon on the Mount, Jesus calls us to rise above self-interest: "Do to others what you would have them do to you."

This call to empathy is part of the narrow road that isn't always popular and is never easy. It requires love and compassion for those who are nothing like us. It needs the courage to look beyond ourselves. For those of us who have the privilege of leading others, whether professionally or personally, and whose decisions impact lives, empathy isn't just a virtue; it's a responsibility. When we step into the shoes of those we lead with humility and understanding, we reflect the very heart of Christ.

—— **Reflection** ——

Who is one person whose shoes you could step into this week by listening a little longer and caring a little deeper?

12. The Only One

"For the Spirit God gave us does not make us timid, but gives us power, love and self-discipline."

(2 Timothy 1:7)

In 2 Timothy 1:7, the apostle Paul encourages Timothy not to be afraid but to embrace the spirit of power, love, and self-discipline that God has given us. Paul was likely facing persecution and imprisonment, which may have made Timothy fearful about sharing the Gospel. This verse serves as a reminder that God's Spirit empowers us to overcome fear and stand firm in our faith, even when it means standing out.

I often encourage my girls to step outside their comfort zones and take on new challenges, even when it makes them stand out like they are the only one in the room. As a mother, I can confidently push them to take a risk and step out of their comfort zone, but it's more challenging for me to do the same. Often, the fear of being negatively perceived by others makes me hold back. I don't want to stand out and be different.

Have you ever experienced this feeling of fear when you stand up for what you believe in? Have you ever had the feeling of being different and being "the only one"?

The only woman in a decision-making environment where the majority of the voices are male? The only Christian at work, and you are asked to make a decision that compromises your ethics? The only student in the classroom who doesn't understand a new concept that everyone else seems to have grasped? The only parent who has a concern with a change that has recently happened in school that impacts your family?

Paul's words in 2 Timothy 1:7 remind us that God has not given us a spirit of fear, but of power, love, and self-discipline. He is always with us, empowering us to embrace our differences and confidently stand in our beliefs.

As you step out in courage, rise above yourself and your feelings and stand firm in the power of God, knowing that you have a spirit of power, love, and self-discipline.

 **Prayer**

God, give me the courage to speak up even when it means I will stand out. Amen.

Section 3

The Human Heart

God loves us deeply, and He cares about how we love ourselves and others. In these devotions, let Him do the gentle heart work.

13. Guard Your Heart

"Above all else, guard your heart, for everything you do flows from it. Keep your mouth free of perversity; keep corrupt talk far from your lips. Let your eyes look straight ahead; fix your gaze directly before you. Give careful thought to the paths for your feet and be steadfast in all your ways."

(Proverbs 4:23–26)

As summer ended and our girls prepared to move from elementary to middle school, I felt a familiar twinge of nervousness. Who would influence them in this new season? Would new friendships strengthen or challenge the values we worked so hard to nurture?

I'm reminded of a moment a few years ago, when one of our daughters came home upset after a friend had called her a bad name. My first instinct was to intervene immediately, call the school to protect her, and fix the situation. But I paused, prayed for wisdom, and listened. Together, we talked through how to respond with grace and courage. That day, I realized guarding the heart isn't about controlling every circumstance; it's about teaching discernment, patience, and trust in God's guidance.

Guarding our hearts is challenging in a world full of distractions, phones, social media, news, and endless opinions. Every platform seems designed to pull our attention in countless directions. How do we keep our gaze fixed on living a Christ-centered life rather than letting the world shape our values and priorities?

It begins with the small choices: what we dwell on, what conversations we engage in, the media we consume, and the boundaries we set. It means pausing before reacting and inviting the Spirit to guide our words, actions, and relationships. By doing so, we model wisdom and discernment for our children not in perfection, but in intentional faith.

When we slow down and keep our eyes forward and find time to seek God, He strengthens our hearts. Our children see our example, and they will learn to do the same.

Prayer

God, we can't be with our children and grandchildren every moment of every day, but You can. Build a fence of protection around them. Amen.

14. Friend-Raising

"One who has unreliable friends soon comes to ruin, but there is a friend who sticks closer than a brother."
(Proverbs 18:24)

I have a genuine love for people, and I cherish the friendships I've made over time. Yet I've learned that not all friendships last a lifetime. Some are only for a season. Each one, however, brings its own joy and happiness during its time.

With maturity comes the realization that joy and happiness flow not only from friends and family but also from friends, coworkers, and acquaintances, both old and new. Community is the key to happiness. Being open to *friend-raising*, a term I recently learned at a women's leadership and philanthropy conference, can be a holy ministry. Extending love and support to others is a way of being a light and bringing people to Christ, even when we don't feel like it or when it takes effort to get to know someone new.

I've seen this echoed by retired coworkers and friends who have discovered new joy in cultivating meaningful connections now that they have more time and their children are grown. Fellowship brings profound love and delight. Proverbs 18:24 reminds us of the value of true, loyal friendship. Unlike superficial companions who may lead us astray, genuine friends offer unwavering support, sometimes even more than family.

Perhaps in your life today, there's a friend from high school or college or someone who has moved away with whom you haven't connected in a while. Maybe it's time to give them a call, catch up, and show that you care. Your gesture of love and attention will likely bring joy, not only to them but to you as well, and it may inspire them to reach out to someone they've been missing too.

Prayer

Lord, thank You for the friends You have placed in every season of my life. Help me nurture meaningful connections and become a friend who reflects Your love. Amen.

15. Are We Just Friends?

"Love the Lord your God with all your heart and with all your soul and with all your mind."

(Matthew 22:37)

There's a difference between friendship and a relationship. A friendship can be supportive, occasional, and comfortable, built on care and trust. But a relationship, especially one rooted in love, requires regular presence, intimacy, commitment, and consistency.

I was reminded of this just last week, when my youngest daughter started summer camp. She chose the same camp as a playmate she met last year, and the two have become very good friends. When her sister teased her about her feelings, she quickly replied, "We're just friends."

That simple phrase stayed with me. It made me wonder: Am I "just friends" with God? Do I check in only when I need something, keeping things casual, surface-level, never going deeper? Or am I in a true relationship with Him, talking daily, sharing my highs and lows, inviting Him into my choices, and making space for His voice in my life?

We choose how close we let God in. Some of us are content staying on casual terms with Him. But

God desires more. He is pursuing more. He wants more than a convenient friendship; He longs for an intimate, committed relationship, in which He is our priority.

That's not always easy. Life pulls us in many directions. Responsibilities, distractions, and fatigue can push God further down the list. But God's love isn't passive. It's intentional. It shows up. It leans in. It prioritizes presence.

As we grow in faith, let's ask ourselves honestly: Are we just friends with God, or are we truly in a relationship with Him? May we choose daily to love Him with all our heart, all our soul, and all our mind.

Prayer

God, help me nurture my relationship with You. Amen.

16. Love Without a Checklist

**"Love is patient, love is kind.
It does not envy, it does not boast,
it is not proud. It does not dishonor
others, it is not self-seeking, it is
not easily angered, it keeps
no record of wrongs."**

(1 Corinthians 13:4–5)

Too fat. Too thin. Too dark. Too light. Too ambitious. Not ambitious enough. Shares too much. Doesn't share enough. The list goes on.

The more I listen to friends and coworkers navigating relationships, the more I see how dating has become like hiring: write a job description, screen candidates, and hope the "perfect fit" shows up. We swipe, evaluate, and move on if one checkbox isn't met.

But what if God leads us to relationships *without* our checklist? What if every person we meet friends, mentors, partners has a purpose we can't see yet?

A college friend once told me, "God chooses the people you need." I laughed then, because I liked feeling in control. Now I know she was right. Some of the most important relationships in my life didn't match the list I thought I needed, but they were exactly what God knew I needed.

Paul's words remind us that God never asked us to evaluate others; He asked us to *love* others. To show patience. To be kind. To let go of pride, of keeping score, of managing and engineering every connection.

So I ask myself often: Am I trusting God to guide my relationships, or am I still clinging to my checklist?

Love isn't a checklist. It's a calling to show grace one relationship at a time.

Reflection

Where might God be inviting you to let go of the checklist and embrace the person He has placed right in front of you?

17. Lonely

"Even though I walk through the darkest valley, I will fear no evil, for you are with me; your rod and your staff, they comfort me."

(Psalm 23:4)

I sat at a crowded coffee shop, surrounded by the hum of conversation, the clinking of cups, and the whir of espresso machines, waiting for a friend. As I watched people laugh and chat, a quiet sadness settled in my chest. In that moment, amid all the noise and life, I felt completely alone. Loneliness can weigh on us heavily, even in a room full of people. This feeling was strange, because I really do enjoy my own company.

Have you ever felt the same? You can have family, friends, and coworkers all around and still feel totally alone. A friend told me they spent three days in the hospital without a single visitor. When I asked why they didn't reach out to me or any of their friends, they said they didn't want to be a burden. They spent those days watching movies, scrolling through social media, and counting the hours until they could leave their room.

Even with faith and community, friends, family,

and community, loneliness can still find us. We crave connection, yet we hesitate to share our needs, afraid it might make us look weak or needy.

Psalm 23:4 reminds us that God is always with us, even in our darkest valleys. But God often works through people as well. We can reach out to the people God has placed in our lives when we need them without being a burden. A short call, a knock on the door, or an invitation for coffee can light up a lonely heart—both theirs and yours. God is present in these small acts. We are never truly alone.

Prayer

Lord, when loneliness creeps in, remind me that You are close. Give me the courage to reach out for connection and the compassion to notice when someone else is feeling lonely. Amen.

18. Unbreakable Love

"For I am convinced that neither death nor life, neither angels nor demons, neither the present nor the future, nor any powers, neither height nor depth, nor anything else in all creation, will be able to separate us from the love of God that is in Christ Jesus our Lord."

(Romans 8:38–39)

Have you ever been reunited with a family member or friend after a long time apart? Do you remember that mix of excitement and nervousness before seeing them again, the anticipation of seeing their face, hearing their voice, talking for hours, and catching up on all that had happened? And have you ever worried that maybe the connection you once had wouldn't feel the same anymore, that time, distance, or the different paths life takes us on might have changed things between you?

As human beings, we long for connection, affection, and enduring care in our relationships. It's a blessing when we find it and a gift when it endures the test of time. I recently had that experience when I reconnected with a dear friend after many years. The moment I heard their voice on the phone, it was as if time had melted away. We talked about our families, our work, and the journeys our lives had taken. When I hung up, I was amazed at how little had changed between us; our bond felt just as it did when we met as teenagers.

But that's not always how it goes. People grow apart, circumstances shift, and the closeness we once felt can fade. There can be disagreements, misunderstandings, or choices that don't align with our beliefs, and we can lose connection. In Romans 8:38, the apostle Paul reminds the Christian church and us that there is one connection that will never weaken, one love that will never fade: God's love.

No mistake you make can diminish it.

No ocean or distance can divide it.

No time, fear, worry, insecurity, or even death can destroy it.

What an incredible gift it is to know that no matter what happens, God's love will always remain. It is constant, unconditional, and unbreakable. Nothing we can do will ever drive it away.

—— **Reflection** ——

If there's an old friend or loved one you haven't spoken to in a while, maybe even for many years, why not pick up the phone and reach out to them? You might find that the connection is still there, just waiting to be renewed.

Section 4

Life Is Challenging

When we are in pain, God seems distant; we question and even curse God. God has not left us; He is right there by our side. Lean into God's strength and power.

19. Who Can Understand It?

**" 'For my thoughts are not
your thoughts, neither are your
ways my ways,' declares the Lord.
'As the heavens are higher than the
earth, so are my ways higher than
your ways and my thoughts
than your thoughts.' "**

(Isaiah 55:8–9)

"Come on, Sophia! You've got this! Your race, your pace! Hang in there, well done!" All of these are encouraging words from a dear running buddy who passed away just weeks before the holidays, after a ten-month journey fighting ALS. In just a few months, my running buddy went from being an active runner, cheerleader, and board member in our community running group to losing the ability to walk, speak, eat, and smile. This debilitating disease is incurable and cannot be explained. ALS slowly shuts down the body until your loved one slips away. Even though he was in a wheelchair during the last few months of his life, my running buddy still attended many races that supported ALS, and he spent time with his beloved wife and daughter and his running group.

Seeing a friend decline was a serious struggle for me and all of us in the running group. I just couldn't understand it why would this happen. Why would God do this to him? I would pray, *Speak to me, God; give me an explanation, a reason! Show me Your healing power; show that You are a healing God. I have faith that You will bring him out, give him new life, revive his body, and make him whole again. I know God heard me, but our friend did not live.*

I needed an explanation. Struggling to understand, wrestling with my faith, all I could come up with was Isaiah's words: " 'For my thoughts are not your thoughts, neither are your ways my ways,' declares the Lord. 'As the heavens are higher than the earth, so are my ways higher than your ways and my thoughts than your thoughts." There would be no explanation, no lightbulb moment; just acceptance and comfort. At times, I still hear his voice, cheering me on with the rest of our running buddies: "You've got this; it's your race! Hang in there! Well done!"

Prayer

Comfort us in our times of grief, Lord. When sorrow feels heavy and loneliness surrounds us, remind us that You are near. Amen.

20. Go Easy

"Come to me, all you who are weary and burdened, and I will give you rest. . . . For my yoke is easy and my burden is light."

(Matthew 11:28, 30)

Team meeting, Board meeting. Parent Teacher Association, Choir. Art class. Soccer. Swimming. Kickboxing. Six thousand steps. Ten thousand steps. Work dinner. Business trip. Repeat. Sound familiar?

For me, the wake-up call came from the smallest voice in my home:

"You're doing too much, Mommy. You're just doing too much. Give yourself a break, Go Easy!"

My face flushed. It took a child to speak the truth I had been ignoring. I was trying to be everything for everyone, and in the process, I had over-scheduled myself into exhaustion. Overburdened, overstretched, and just plain weary.

Yes, my husband had kindly said it before, but this time, the innocence of a child's voice cut through my excuses. I knew I had to make a change. Set boundaries. Start saying no.

Jesus doesn't wait for us to collapse before He invites us to rest. He whispers every day: "Come to

Me when you're tired." "Let me carry this with you."

We treat rest like a reward for finishing the list, but what if rest is the starting point? What if giving our burdens to Jesus first is the key to getting through the day?

Being yoked with Him means we don't carry the weight alone. We can go easier on ourselves. Even when we drop the ball, we know He will never drop us.

Reflection

Where in your life do you need to slow down and allow God to give you rest?

21. He's Not Done

"Being confident of this, that he who began a good work in you will carry it on to completion until the day of Christ Jesus."

(Philippians 1:6)

Society often tells us when we should reach life's milestones: childhood, education, career, marriage, children, retirement. But life rarely follows a perfect schedule. Careers shift, marriages don't happen, children never come, and dreams are delayed. Loss, heartbreak, and unexpected changes can leave us questioning our worth.

I recently met with friends quietly carrying the ache of being unmarried and childless. Listening to them reminded me how easily we fall into the trap of comparison. And yet, God's promises are never bound by our timeline. Even in the darkest seasons, He is at work, and there is always a dawn after dusk. I sensed their pain, but I also reminded them that God's plans are still unfolding. I trust that God has a plan for their lives, and I have faith that He will meet the desires of their hearts.

Philippians 1:6 assures us that God is not finished with us. His timing is perfect, and every detour, delay, or disappointment can be a divine redirection. If you ever wonder whether it's too late to begin again to pursue a dream, a new calling, or a relationship, remember that the One who began a good work in you will be faithful to complete it, in His perfect time.

Prayer

God, I believe You have started a good work in me, and I trust that You will complete it. Amen.

22. God Knows

"If any of you lacks wisdom, you should ask God, who gives generously to all without finding fault, and it will be given to you."

(James 1:5)

Over the years, I have evolved professionally, from leading a small team to running a department. The transition was exciting, but it was terrifying too. On my second day as department head, I came home completely overwhelmed.

My husband, calm as ever, looked at me and said, "You've got this. You are qualified, you have everything it takes, and you are equal to the task." But inside, I wasn't so sure. Doubt crept in, and I felt like a fraud. I recall leading a meeting where everyone looked to me for answers, but I didn't have them. I couldn't think on the spot, and I wasn't sure what to say. That's when the weight of fear really hit me. I had to learn fast, adapt quickly, and become comfortable enough to admit when I didn't have the answers.

A few days later, my sister-in-law gave me advice I'll never forget:

"Before your day starts, close your door and ask

God to lead you and give you wisdom for the day." So I did.

I began starting each morning with a few quiet moments, just me and God. That practice didn't make every challenge disappear, but it changed how I carried them. I realized I didn't need to have all the answers; I just needed to stay connected to the One who does.

James reminds us that when we lack wisdom, we can ask for it. God doesn't find fault in our questions or our weakness; He delights in guiding us.

Maybe you've felt the same pressure I did to have all the answers, to appear confident, to hold everything together. Whether you're a parent juggling responsibility, a manager guiding a team, a teacher leading a classroom, or someone just trying to make the next right decision, remember this: you're not expected to do it all in your own strength.

God's wisdom is available for every meeting, every conversation, every moment of uncertainty. We don't have to pretend to have it all figured out. We can lean on the people God places around us for support, and more importantly, we can lean on Him.

Reflection

What situation in your life is calling you to admit, "God, I need Your wisdom here"?

23. Stay in the Race

"I have seen something else under the sun: The race is not to the swift or the battle to the strong, nor does food come to the wise or wealth to the brilliant or favor to the learned; but time and chance happen to them all."

(Ecclesiastes 9:11)

**"But the one who stands firm
to the end will be saved."**

(Matthew 24:13)

In the 2025 New York City Marathon, 59,662 runners started the race, and 59,226 finished. That means 436 runners did not finish: approximately 0.73 percent of all who started. Less than 1 percent dropped out, which means the overwhelming majority endured until the end.*

Most marathoners train for months, beginning with short runs, increasing distance week by week,

* Clément Laborieux, "The Key Numbers Behind the 2025 New York City Marathon: A Record-Breaking Edition," Marathons.com, March 11, 2025, https://www. marathons.com/en/save-the-date/the-key-numbers-behind-the-2025-new-york-city-marathon-a-record-breaking-edition

building stamina, and challenging themselves mentally. And most don't train alone; they train with friends, running groups, and running buddies, because community helps you go farther than you could ever go alone.

In Ecclesiastes 9:11, King Solomon teaches us that you can train, plan, hustle, strategize, and prepare, but life will not always unfold according to your plan. The fastest don't always win. The strongest don't always succeed. The wisest don't always give the best advice. Life can surprise you. Detours, delays, setbacks, and disappointments are part of every journey. No one is immune to this.

But Matthew 24:13 gives us our anchor: "The one who stands firm to the end will be saved."

Perseverance matters. Staying in the race matters. Not because you are the fastest, smartest, or strongest, but because God is with you and you are becoming stronger. You will go through cramps, fatigue, heartbreak, silence, and seasons during which you don't think you can take one more step and you want to quit.

Whether you are training for a literal marathon, searching for employment, waiting for a life partner, starting a family, rebuilding after loss, beginning retirement, or going through another season of waiting, know this: The race is not for the swift nor the battle for the strong but for those who endure until the end.

—— **Reflection** ——

Where do you need endurance today, and who can come alongside you as you continue the race?

59

24. Job Seeker

"But seek first his kingdom and his righteousness, and all these things will be given to you as well."

(Matthew 6:33)

A friend recently called me, overwhelmed by the job market. She had been let go two months ago, and during her job search she had received several rejections. Her confidence was shaken. As she spoke, I heard the weight in her voice of the fear of the unknown, the pressure to find a role where she could make a meaningful impact, and the desire to remain a fully present wife and mother to her two children.

We've journeyed through our careers together for over twenty years. We started as assistants, worked our way through middle management, and now both serve in senior leadership. Yet even though she had decades of experience and an MBA, discouragement crept in. Seasons like this can make even the strongest among us question our worth.

As I listened, I didn't have perfect advice. But the words of the old song came to mind: "Seek ye first the kingdom of God and His righteousness, and all these things shall be added unto you."

It sounds simple, but we know it's not always

easy. We don't know what the next job will be, but we do know God has a job in store. God's got us, and we have our faith.

Job searching can consume your thoughts, drain your time, and make you irritable and grouchy. Scrolling postings, waiting for responses, refreshing your inbox, preparing for interviews. It demands time, energy, and emotional resilience. And yet Jesus invites us to shift our focus. Not to ignore our responsibilities, but to remember who the true Provider is. "His righteousness" simply means aligning our hearts with Him and seeking what pleases God above what pressures us.

Maybe you are job searching. Maybe you are waiting, hoping, praying for something to break, and you can't see how things will work out. God is not silent, and He has not you. Continue to seek Him first, and He forgotten will add everything else to your life.

Prayer

Lord, remind me that my identity is not rooted in a title or a paycheck but in You. Guide every step of my search, and help me seek You first in all things. Open the right doors at the right time, and give me peace while I wait. Amen.

Section 5

Childlike Wonder

Jesus invites us to experience life with childlike wonder: to dream, to laugh, to sing, to shout, and to have faith.

25. Naughty or Nice

"For it is by grace you have been saved, through faith—and this is not from yourselves, it is the gift of God—not by works, so that no one can boast."

(Ephesians 2:8–9)

"She's mean! It's not fair! I know you're not going to get anything from Santa this year, and I can prove it!" That was my youngest daughter, yelling at her older sister. Before I could intervene, she was already tapping furiously on her laptop, typing in names as fast as her little fingers could move. Seconds later, she proudly read the screen aloud:

"Naughty! Neatness needs improvement. Behavior has been good sometimes, not so good other times. Manners could still use some attention. Was nice last Monday.'"

Then she turned to her sister with the triumphant confidence only a youngest child can have: "See? I told you! You're on the naughty list!"

It wasn't even mid-November, and the Santa naughty-or-nice website* as well as the Santa tracker were already up and running. Kids every-

* The Naughty and Nice List 2025 website, https://www.christmasaffairs.com/list/

where were checking the status of their siblings and friends, deciding who would or would not receive Christmas presents this year. On the screen was Santa himself, complete with a barometer labeled Not Nice, Sorta Nice, and Nice—a whole system dedicated to rating behavior.

As I watched, two thoughts crossed my mind: *Should I type my name in?* and *Does God have a record like this for us?* Does He keep a running tally of how often we've been naughty or nice? If that's the case, oh boy, I'm in trouble. Because if I'm honest, some weeks, especially around this time of year, I am not nice.

But here's the freedom Paul reminds us of in Ephesians 2:8–9: Salvation is not based on our good deeds. It is not earned by perfect behavior, neatness, kindness, consistency, or any streak of being good. It is the priceless gift of God, received through faith in Jesus Christ.

Thank God, He does not operate like Santa's naughty-or-nice list.

Later that evening, I turned to my older daughter, the one who found herself on Santa's naughty list, and said, "Do you know something? There's still time. There's always time to turn things around. At any moment, you can choose kindness and love toward your friends and family. And whatever you've done, God can help you start fresh; He's certainly forgiven my sins and helped me start fresh a million times over."

Prayer

Thank You, God, for Your loving kindness. Amen.

26. When Santa Brings Hope

"Blessed are those who mourn,
for they will be comforted."

(Matthew 5:4)

After a long season of illness and many challenges, my father passed away on his birthday, just two weeks before Christmas. Even though we knew the end was coming, the news still landed heavily. As Christmas drew closer, a quiet fear settled deep in my heart.

How could I continue our family traditions without him? How could I get through Christmas morning without breaking down?

In His Sermon on the Mount, Jesus tells us that those who mourn are blessed because they will be comforted. But in the thick of grief, those words feel distant and unreachable. Comfort felt impossible. I didn't want comfort from Jesus or anyone and I didn't want to celebrate Christmas.

On Christmas Eve, we followed our usual routine. We tracked Santa's journey from New Zealand to Australia, Africa to Europe, and finally across the ocean to North America yes, even to New York City.*

* Google Santa Tracker website, https://santatracker.google.com/.>

We set out cookies and milk. But when Christmas day arrived, my heart was still mournful.

Then my youngest daughter burst into the room.

"Mommy! The cookies are gone! The milk is finished! Santa came! Come downstairs—you have to see!" So much joy, so much hope. So much belief.

I wiped my eyes, climbed out of bed, and followed her downstairs. In that moment, her joy lifted me. It reminded me of something I had forgotten: grief and joy can exist side by side.

Santa brought excitement, but God brought comfort. He carried my sorrow when I couldn't and gave me grace for Christmas when I didn't feel ready.

Sometimes, the hope we need comes through the wide-eyed faith of a child and the gentle presence of a Savior who never leaves us in our grief.

Reflection

Where might God be offering you small glimpses of comfort in this season of loss?

27. His Eyes Are Everywhere

"Where can I go from your Spirit?
Where can I flee from your presence?
If I go up to the heavens, you are
there; if I make my bed in the depths,
you are there. If I rise on the wings of
the dawn, if I settle on the far side of
the sea, even there your hand
will guide me, your right hand
will hold me fast."

(Psalm 139:7–10)

Did you have a parent who made you feel like you couldn't get away with anything? I certainly did. My parents would often say that God is "the silent listener to every conversation and the unseen guest at every meal." I didn't understand it fully at the time, but I believed it wholeheartedly. Whenever I tried to do something in secret, my mother *already knew*. Sometimes I thought she could read my mind!

Psalm 139 captures that feeling perfectly. There is no place beyond God's reach. Whether we soar to the heavens or hide in the deepest darkness, He is there—guiding, comforting, watching, and lovingly protecting.

That truth shaped my childhood. God wasn't distant; He was everywhere.

And now, as a mother myself, I find those very words coming out of my own mouth. Recently, our children started middle school and began traveling to and from school independently. We asked them to come straight home afterward, but of course curiosity and independence got the best of them. When they assured me they had followed directions, I gently let them know that both God and I knew they had taken a detour to the store.

"How did you know?" they asked.

I smiled and said, "Oh, I had a cup of coffee with God this afternoon, and He told me everything." (What I didn't tell them was that the chocolate wrapper in the trash gave them away!)

Reflection

Where do you need to be reminded that God is present and guiding you, even when you can't see Him?

28. The Joneses

"For where you have envy and selfish ambition, there you find disorder and every evil practice. But the wisdom that comes from heaven is first of all pure; then peace-loving, considerate, submissive, full of mercy and good fruit, impartial and sincere."

(James 3:16–17)

In today's world, our twenty-four-hour days can so quickly be swallowed up by coffee, commutes, kids, work, dinner, laundry, late-night emails, and endless errands. By the time the day ends, we've often given everything else our best, and God just the leftover minutes.

I don't know about you, but sometimes I feel like I'm running in a rat race, trying not just to keep up but to be the best. And in that striving, I've caught myself envying others, wishing I had what they had, or longing to be someone else.

Maybe you've felt it too, scrolling through friends' summer vacation photos, or when you're struggling with finances or problems at work, while your neighbor's life seems flawless and carefree.

Jealousy blinds us. It whispers that God's design for our lives isn't enough, that we need more.

But that is not true. God's design for us is His wisdom, His plan.

"But the wisdom that comes from heaven is first of all pure; then peace-loving, considerate, submissive, full of mercy and good fruit, impartial and sincere" (James 3:17).

God's Word reminds us that what He has placed in us is good, whole, intentional, and perfect. Jealousy may be a natural emotion, but when we turn our eyes back to God and choose gratitude, jealousy loses its grip.

Reflection

Where do you need to turn your eyes away from others and back to God?

29. You're Forgiven

"For if you forgive other people when they sin against you, your heavenly Father will also forgive you. But if you do not forgive others, your Father will not forgive your sins."

(Matthew 6:14–15)

"I'm gonna tell! If you don't do it, I'm going to tell not just about this time, but about all the other times!"

"That's not fair! That's blackmail!"

I stood on the stairs, listening to my daughters use past wrongs as leverage to get what they wanted. I wondered what they could have done that was so terrible they felt the need to store it away like ammunition.

So I asked gently, "What did you do that is so bad you can't tell me?"

My daughter insisted she couldn't share, because I would be so angry that I would never forgive her. I assured her that no matter what it was, we could work through it together. She could tell me the truth. I would forgive her. Her slate could be wiped clean, and she could start fresh.

In that moment, I remembered how many times my mother forgave me growing up for the lies, the sneaking around, the childish mistakes that seemed like the end of the world at the time. And yet, forgiveness always made room for restoration.

Forgiveness is something we all wrestle with. Sometimes holding onto a grudge feels easier than letting go. But Jesus teaches us in Matthew 6:14–15 that forgiveness isn't optional: it's a calling. He forgives us, and He expects us to extend that same grace to others.

Maybe today you are carrying the weight of a grudge you've held for years. Maybe you said you forgave someone, but deep down, the bitterness is still there.

Forgiveness isn't easy. It takes humility, courage, and the strength only God can provide. But when we choose to forgive, we release others and ourselves into the freedom God intends.

Reflection

Who do you need to release from the "record of wrongs" you've been holding onto?

30. Shout

"When the trumpets sounded, the army shouted, and at the sound of the trumpet, when the men gave a loud shout, the wall collapsed."

(Joshua 6:20)

I hold tightly to the promise that all things work together for good and that God is leading me even when I can't see the full picture. I try to stay positive and look for the best in every situation. But there are times when life feels deeply disheartening. Some seasons are heavy, dark, and discouraging, and I feel like losing hope.

Recently, a close friend from childhood lost her mother. I had known her mom for over thirty years. Listening to my friend describe the pain of that loss was heart-wrenching. As I sat with her, holding space and offering comfort, I did my best to stay composed and positive. I didn't want to cry in front of her. I didn't want to shout at God and ask why he had forsaken my friend.

But the truth is, sometimes the pressure builds. And I *do* need to shout and cry at God.

Sometimes out of rage. Sometimes as a release.

It's a shout of grief that transforms into a spiritual cry, a deep, guttural sound that comes from faith, desperation, and sometimes sheer exhaustion. It's the kind of shout you let out when you've prayed, waited, worked, and endured, and now, by faith, you're declaring victory *before* the result even shows up.

It reminds me of Joshua and the Israelites. For six days, they walked silently around the walls of Jericho. No complaints. No chatter. Just quiet, obedient faith. But on the seventh day, God gave them a new instruction: *Shout.* It wasn't random. It was purposeful, divinely timed, and powerful. The shout didn't just express emotion. It ushered in the miracle.

Sometimes God calls us to stillness. Other times, He invites us to raise our voices and *shout.*

Prayer

Thank You, God, for staying close in every season, both the quiet and the loud. When the pressure builds, give me the courage to shout out to You. Amen.

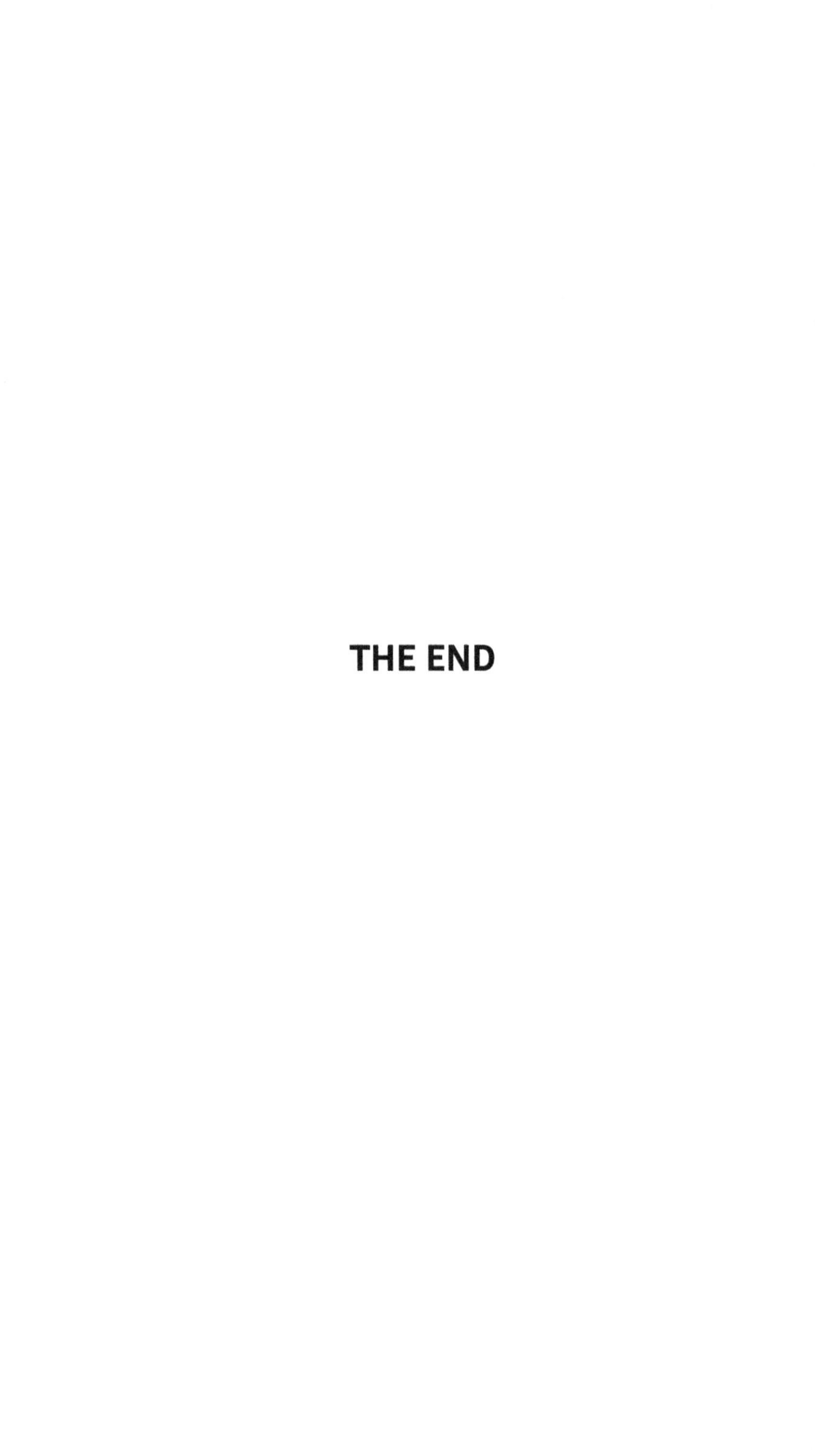

THE END

Notes

Notes

Notes

Notes

Notes

Notes

About the Author

Sophia May is a faith-centered leader, deacon, writer, and encourager with a heart for community and service. She serves as a mission-driven human resources executive at a nonprofit in New York City, where she champions a culture of servant leadership and employee development and well-being.

A pastor's daughter raised in England, Sophia later relocated to the United States to begin her career in journalism. Today, she captures everyday moments with warmth, honesty, and humor, using Scripture to illuminate God's love and guidance.

She holds a bachelor of arts in media production, a master of arts in radio journalism, and a master of science in human resources management, bringing depth in storytelling and leadership insight to her work and ministry.

Sophia lives in New York with her husband and their three children. Her family, friends, and colleagues inspire many of her devotions. *God, Me, and Coffee* is her first devotional book, written with gratitude, laughter, tears, and many cups of coffee.

9 798995 077107